CREATE YOUR NOW

SIMPLE STEPS TO CRAFT THE LIFE YOU WANT

JAYESH CHOPADE

Contents

Preface

Life often feels like a whirlwind of expectations, responsibilities, and unrelenting noise. We chase after goals, navigate challenges, and try to make sense of it all—only to feel like we're falling short, stuck, or lost. I know this feeling intimately because I've been there.

Create Your Now is not just a book; it's a reflection of my journey. It's a story of wrestling with self-doubt, struggling with indecision, and learning how to rise from setbacks. More importantly, it's about discovering the profound power of the present moment—embracing it fully and using it as a launchpad to create a life of purpose and intention.

I wrote this book because I believe that we all have the power to change the trajectory of our lives, no matter where we are starting from. But that change doesn't come from waiting for the perfect moment, overthinking, or clinging to the past. It comes from recognizing that now is all we truly have, and within it lies infinite potential.

In these pages, I've poured my personal experiences—the triumphs, the mistakes, and the lessons that shaped who I am today. This isn't a manual filled with theories or a roadmap for someone else's life. It's a candid account of my journey, shared with the hope that it will inspire you to embark on your own.

You'll find stories of my turning points, practical strategies that worked for me, and moments that made me pause and rethink everything. My aim is not to tell you what to do, but to spark a realization within you: that you have everything it takes to create your now.

As you read, I encourage you to approach this book with an open mind and heart. Reflect on the experiences I share, relate them to your own, and see how they might guide you toward living more intentionally.

This book is my story, but its purpose is you.

So, let's begin this journey together—starting now.
With gratitude and hope,
Jayesh

Introduction

Have you ever felt like life is running ahead of you, and no matter how hard you try, you can't seem to catch up? I've been there—stuck in that loop of wanting to do more, be more, and live more, but constantly feeling like time, opportunity, or maybe even myself was holding me back.

For years, I was waiting. Waiting for the perfect moment, the right circumstances, or some magical sign to start living the life I dreamed of. But here's the truth: those perfect moments never arrived. What did arrive were unexpected challenges, self-doubt, and an overwhelming feeling that maybe this was all life had to offer.

The turning point came when I stopped waiting and started acting. And that's where this book begins.
Create Your Now is not a guide to perfection. It's not about having all the answers or creating a flawless life. It's about making the most of what you have right now and using it as a foundation to build something extraordinary. This is not a theory I read about in a book or learned in a seminar—it's the essence of what I've lived.

This book is deeply personal because the lessons in these pages were forged in my own struggles. I'm not here to preach, and I'm certainly not here to pretend I've figured it all out. What I do know is this: when I stopped waiting for the future to fix itself and took ownership of my present, everything began to change.

We live in a world that constantly pulls us in different directions—toward achievements, social comparisons, and endless distractions. But amidst all this noise, there's a quiet truth: you have the power to shape your life. And that power lies in the decisions you make and the actions you take right now.

In this book, I'll share with you the experiences that transformed my lifetimes when I stumbled, moments when I learned, and choices that redefined my path. Along the way, I'll invite you to reflect on your own journey and explore practical ways to create a life that feels meaningful and true to you.

This is not just about changing your circumstances; it's about shifting your perspective, embracing your power, and realizing that the smallest step today can spark a profound transformation tomorrow. My hope is that Create Your Now will be more than a book you read. I hope it will feel like a conversation with a friend—one who's been where you are and wants nothing more than to see you thrive.

The journey starts here, at this moment. And the best part? It's yours to create.

Let's begin.
Jayesh

Prologue

Setting the Stage: Understanding the Power of Now

Imagine this: you and I are sitting on a cozy balcony, sipping chai or coffee—your pick. The breeze is cool, and the conversation flows easily, the way it always does with good friends.

"*So, tell me,*" you ask, leaning back in your chair, "*what's the deal with this whole living in the now thing? It sounds like one of those motivational quotes that everyone shares but no one really follows.*"

I laugh because, honestly, I've been there too—rolling my eyes at all the Instagram posts telling me to seize the day while I scroll through them, procrastinating on something important. "*Yeah,*" I reply, grinning, "*it sounds cheesy, right? But hear me out—it's not just some feel-good fluff. It's real, and it's powerful.*"

Here's the thing about now. It's all we really have. Not to sound like a philosopher, but think about it—yesterday? Gone. Tomorrow? Not guaranteed. All the things we want to do, the changes we dream about, the life we hope to build—it all starts with what we choose to do right now.

I remember a time when this idea hit me hard. It was one of those days when I felt completely stuck. Work was overwhelming, I was behind on my goals, and instead of tackling any of it, I was binge-watching a series I didn't even like that much. A friend called me—let's call him Amit—and said something that made me pause.

"*Bro,*" he said, "*what are you doing?*"

"Chilling," I replied, which was code for avoiding life. *"Chilling? Really? Or are you hiding from the stuff you actually need to do?"*

Ouch. He wasn't wrong. And that's the beauty of friends—they'll call you out, not because they want to hurt you, but because they want to see you grow. That day, I decided to stop avoiding and start acting. And you know what? It felt terrifying, but it also felt empowering.

The power of now isn't about doing everything perfectly or suddenly transforming into this hyper-productive superhero. It's about recognizing that this moment—this very second—is your chance to take one small step. Maybe it's sending that email you've been putting off, making that call, or simply deciding that today, you're going to try.

"Okay, but how do you stay in the now when life keeps throwing curveballs?" you ask, raising an eyebrow.

Great question. Life will always throw curveballs—that's kind of its thing. But staying in the now doesn't mean ignoring your problems or pretending everything's fine. It means focusing on what you can do instead of stressing over what you can't control.

It's like this: Imagine you're driving on a foggy road. You can't see the entire path ahead, but you can see a few feet in front of you. That's enough to keep moving, right? That's the power of now—taking it one moment, one step, one decision at a time.

And here's the best part—when you start acting in the now, no matter how small those actions are, you create momentum. That momentum builds, and suddenly, you're not just thinking about change—you're living it.

"So, what's your now?" I ask, leaning forward with a smile. *"What's that one thing you can do today to move closer to where you want to be?"*

You pause, thinking it over, and I can see that spark of realization in your eyes. And that's when I know—we've just set the stage for something incredible.

It's your turn now. Let's create it together.

How This Book Came to Be

Let me tell you a story—because you're my friend, and friends get the behind-the-scenes scoop.

It all started during one of those random late-night conversations that seem to solve all of life's problems (or at least make you feel like you've solved them until morning). My friend Amol and I were sitting in his tiny living room, surrounded by empty pizza boxes and an alarming number of coffee mugs. He looked at me, half-serious, half-joking, and said, *"Jayesh, you've got to stop just talking about these ideas and start writing them down. Seriously, write a book or something!"*

"A book?" I laughed, nearly choking on my cold coffee. *"Amol, you've seen my to-do list. Adding write a book to it would probably make it combust."*

"Exactly!" he said, pointing his slice of pizza at me like it was a magic wand. *"You're always telling us about your experiences and how you turned things around. You've helped me figure out my mess—why not help more people? Besides, you're always talking anyway; might as well put it on paper."*

He wasn't wrong, though. My friends had heard it all—the stories of my bad decisions, the times I'd been stuck, and the small, sometimes ridiculous steps I'd taken to get unstuck. Like that one time I set 20 alarms to make sure I woke up early for a morning jog...and still slept through 18 of them. The point was, I'd learned, adapted, and found ways to keep moving forward.

The idea of writing it all down didn't leave me. Over the next few days, I started scribbling notes on whatever I could find—sticky notes, the back of receipts, even my phone screen.

I'd jot down things like: *"Remember to write about that time you almost gave up but didn't."* Or *"Explain why deciding to start is the hardest but most important step."*

But here's the funny part—I didn't realize I was writing a book at first. It felt more like journaling or storytelling. I'd write about something that happened, how I handled it, what I learned, and what I'd do differently. And the more I wrote, the more I started seeing patterns—things that worked for me that might work for others too.

One day, Amol called me again. *"So, how's the combustible to-do list going?"* he asked, teasing.

"Actually, I started writing," I admitted. *"But it's not a book yet—it's more like me rambling to myself on paper."*

"That's a start!" he said, laughing. *"Remember, no one expects perfection. Just keep going. And don't forget to add that story about the alarms—you've got to let people know they're not the only ones who fail miserably sometimes."*

And that's exactly what I did. This book grew from those scribbled notes, late-night talks, and countless moments of figuring out life one small step at a time. It's not about me being an expert or having all the answers—I'm just like you, navigating through this journey called life.

This book isn't polished wisdom handed down from some mountaintop. It's messy, real, and honest—just like life. I wanted it to feel like we're sitting together, laughing at my missteps, learning from my wins, and figuring things out together.

So, here it is: my story, my lessons, and my journey—written for you. Not because I have it all figured out, but because I believe in sharing what we know, hoping it helps someone else.

And honestly? If Amol were here right now, he'd probably raise a coffee mug and say, *"Cheers to that!"* So, cheers to us—for being here, for showing up, and for starting something new.

Let's dive in.

CHAPTER ONE

MY WAKE-UP CALL

So, where were we? Oh right, chai, Amol, and my mini financial crisis. That was just the beginning.

You know those moments in life when you realize that everything you've been doing so far needs a serious overhaul? Yeah, this was one of those. It wasn't just about my bank balance (although, let's be real, that was a pretty big nudge). It was about everything—my habits, my mindset, my ability to procrastinate like it was an Olympic sport.

Let me rewind a bit. After that initial wake-up call, Amol and I started having these long conversations about, well, everything. He's the kind of friend who'll roast you mercilessly but still stick around to help you figure things out. And honestly, those talks became my therapy sessions.

One evening, we were sitting in our usual spot—a small roadside café that served the best vada pav and cutting chai in the city. I was rambling about how I felt like I'd been sleepwalking through life.

"I mean, how did I even get here, Amol? It's like I've been on autopilot for years," I said, dunking a biscuit into my chai and watching it disintegrate.

"You got here one takeout order and one Netflix binge at a time," he said, smirking. "But seriously, Jayesh, you're not alone. Most people don't even realize they're on autopilot until they crash into something. At least you've figured it out before total disaster."

"Comforting," I said, rolling my eyes. *"But you're right. I need to stop coasting and start driving, even if I don't know the destination yet."*

"That's the spirit!" Amol said, raising his vada pav like a toast. *"Here's to figuring it out, one slightly messy step at a time."*

And that's exactly what I did—or at least tried to do. The next morning, I sat down with a notebook (yes, an actual, physical notebook because I needed this to feel serious) and started writing down everything I wanted to change. My finances were the obvious starting point, but as I wrote, I realized it went deeper than that.

It was about the little choices I was making every day—the ones that seemed insignificant at the time but added up to a life that didn't quite feel like mine. Skipping workouts, hitting snooze, saying "I'll start tomorrow" to just about everything. It was time to flip the script.

And let me tell you, the first few days of *"living intentionally"* were...interesting.

Like, I remember deciding to wake up early one morning and go for a jog. I texted Amol, feeling all proud of myself, and he responded with, *"Who are you, and what have you done with the real Jayesh?"*When I actually showed up at his place in jogging shoes, he nearly dropped his cup of coffee. *"Wow, miracles do happen,"* he said, laughing. *"But let's see if you survive beyond day one."*
Spoiler: I barely did. Halfway through the jog, I was wheezing like an old harmonium, and Amol had to bribe me with chai to keep me moving.

"See?" he said, grinning. *"Progress already. You're running and motivated by chai. That's called balance."*

But here's the thing—it was progress. Tiny, awkward, often hilarious progress, but progress nonetheless. And that's what I want you to take away from this. Wake-up calls aren't about fixing everything overnight. They're about realizing you can fix things—and then taking that first step, no matter how small or ridiculous it feels.

So, friend, what's your wake-up call? And if you're not sure yet, don't worry—it's coming. When it does, I'll be here, cheering you on, chai in hand.

The Moment That Changed Everything

So, there I was, slowly piecing my life together, one chai-fueled decision at a time. Things were moving, albeit at the speed of a snail on a rainy day. I thought I had everything under control. Thought is the keyword. Because then came the moment. You know, the kind that flips your world upside down and leaves you wondering, *"What just happened?"*

It started as an ordinary day. I had plans to meet Amol for our usual chai-and-chatter session. He called it chai therapy, and honestly, it worked better than most self-help books.

"Jayesh," Amol said, sliding into his chair at the café, *"you won't believe what just happened at work."*
"Let me guess," I said, stirring my chai. *"You finally learned how to use Excel without asking your intern?"*
"Hilarious," he shot back, rolling his eyes. *"No, this is serious. My manager called me in for a one-on-one, and we ended up talking about life goals. Do you have any idea how awkward it is to tell someone you've never thought about your life beyond Friday evenings and paydays?"*

I laughed, but his words stuck with me. That night, as I lay staring at my ceiling, I realized I wasn't much better off. Sure, I'd started making small changes, but when it came to the bigger picture? Blank slate.

Then came the real moment. A few days later, I was scrolling through social media—mindlessly, as one does—when I came across a video of a man in his sixties running a marathon. The caption read: *"It's never too late to rewrite your story."*

And just like that, something clicked.

"Amol," I texted, *"have you ever seen a 60-year-old run a marathon?"*

He replied almost instantly. *"Only in movies. Why? Are you planning to sign up for one? Should I alert the ambulance in advance?"*

"Very funny," I shot back. *"No, it just got me thinking. What's stopping us from doing something big? Like really big? Something that scares the hell out of us but also makes us feel alive?"*

Amol, ever the skeptic, replied, *"Define 'big.' Because if you're talking about bungee jumping, I'm out. Gravity and I have an agreement."*

"No," I said, laughing. *"I'm serious. What if we stopped coasting and started living? Like, truly living. What if we gave ourselves permission to chase the crazy, impossible things?"*

He didn't reply for a while, and I figured he was done humoring me. But then my phone buzzed.

"Okay," he said. *"Let's do it. But don't blame me if we end up broke or in traction."*

That was it—the moment that changed everything. It wasn't the marathon video itself. It was the idea it sparked: that life doesn't have to be a series of safe, predictable steps. It can be messy, bold, and downright terrifying—and that's exactly what makes it worth living.

From that point on, my perspective shifted. I started asking myself bigger questions: What do I really want? What's stopping me from going after it? And perhaps most importantly, what will it take for me to look back one day and say, *"Yeah, I really lived"*?

Friend, I hope this chapter inspires you to find your own *"moment."* Maybe it's already happened, or maybe it's just around the corner. Either way, trust me—it's worth paying attention. And when it hits? Oh boy, get ready, because life as you know it is about to get a whole lot more interesting.

Recognizing the Need for Change

So, after that marathon guy lit a fire in my brain, I started paying attention to everything in my life. And when I say everything, I mean even the stuff I usually ignored—like the mountain of unread books on my shelf, the fitness app I'd downloaded but never opened, and, oh yeah, my bank balance.

Amol and I were catching up at our usual chai spot when I brought it up.

"Amol," I said, leaning back in my chair, *"do you ever feel like life is... I don't know, stagnant?"*

He raised an eyebrow. *"Stagnant? You're getting poetic, Jayesh. Next thing you'll tell me you're writing haikus about your morning toast."*

"I'm serious, man," I said, throwing a sugar packet at him. *"I mean, don't you think we're stuck in this loop? Work, eat, scroll, sleep, repeat?"*

Amol took a sip of his chai and nodded thoughtfully. *"You might be onto something. But here's the thing: loops are comfortable. Change? That's messy. Who wants to deal with messy?"*

"Messy is where the magic happens," I replied, with all the confidence of someone quoting a motivational poster.

He snorted. *"Alright, Mr. Magic, what are you planning to do? Meditate on a mountain? Move to Goa and become a yoga instructor?"*

"Not quite," I said, laughing. *"But I do think we need to stop waiting for life to change on its own. It's like... we're passengers in our own story, you know?"*

That conversation stayed with me. Later that night, as I stared at the ceiling again (yes, the ceiling and I were having a lot of deep moments lately), I realized how easy it is to settle into routines. You tell yourself you're just waiting for the right time. But then days turn into months, and suddenly, you're looking at years.

Here's the thing: recognizing the need for change isn't always about having some dramatic moment of clarity. Sometimes, it's the small, nagging feeling that you're meant for something more. It's the quiet frustration when you realize you're surviving, not thriving.

For me, it was little things—like feeling envious of people who seemed genuinely excited about their lives or catching myself making excuses for why I hadn't started that project or learned that skill.

I called Amol the next day. *"Okay, I think I've figured it out,"* I said.
"Figured what out?" he asked, half-distracted.

"Why we don't change, even when we know we need to."
"Oh, this should be good," he said, feigning interest. "Enlighten me, guruji."
"It's because change feels like a chore," I explained. "Like something we have to do instead of something we get to do. It's all in how we frame it."
Amol paused. "That's... actually not bad," he admitted. "So, what's your big plan?"
"My plan," I said, grinning, "is to stop overthinking and start doing. No big declarations, no waiting for the perfect moment. Just small, deliberate steps toward something better."

Friend, if you've ever felt that itch—that quiet voice telling you there's more out there for you—listen to it. It doesn't matter how messy or scary change seems. What matters is recognizing it's time and deciding you're worth the effort.

Because trust me, the moment you embrace the idea that you get to rewrite your story, everything starts to shift. And when it does? Oh, the places you'll go—and the chai you'll drink along the way.

Key Takeaways

1. The Moment That Changed Everything

- This chapter discusses a pivotal moment when everything shifted for the author, realizing that life wasn't aligning with personal goals or desires.
- It highlights the power of a wake-up call, a moment of frustration, or feeling stuck that pushes one to recognize the need for change.

2. Recognizing the Need for Change

- The chapter emphasizes how recognizing the need for change is often the first step toward transformation.
- It encourages the reader to reflect on their own life and identify areas where they feel stagnant or unfulfilled, as this awareness is key to moving forward.

Homework

- Reflect on moments when you've felt stuck or frustrated. What patterns do you notice?
- Identify one area of your life where change is needed.
- Write down one small action step to take today that will move you toward the change you desire.

CHAPTER TWO

BREAKING THE MIND CAGE

You know that moment when you realize the biggest thing holding you back isn't your circumstances, but your own thoughts? Yeah, it's a hard pill to swallow. For me, this realization hit like a truck one lazy Sunday afternoon.

I was scrolling through social media—classic doom-scrolling—when I came across a post that said, "Your mind can be your greatest ally or your worst enemy." Normally, I'd just roll my eyes at something so cliché, but this time, it hit differently. Probably because I'd spent weeks wrestling with self-doubt and procrastination.

Think about it. How many times do we trap ourselves in this invisible cage of *"I'm not good enough," "What if I fail?"* or the classic, *"It's too late for me to try"*? It's like having a personal jailer living rent-free in your head.

I realized I had built an imaginary wall around myself, and every time I tried to climb over it, my brain went, *"Nope, you can't do that."*

We spend so much energy overanalyzing our limitations instead of challenging them.

So, I decided to take a closer look at my so-called "mind cage." What were the bars made of? For me, it was fear of failure, a bad habit of comparing myself to others, and this overwhelming need for everything to be perfect before I even started.

Sound familiar?

Here's the thing: breaking the mind cage isn't about bulldozing through life with blind optimism. It's about getting honest with yourself—identifying the fears, habits, and beliefs that are keeping you locked up. And let me tell you, it's not always pretty.

One of my biggest breakthroughs came when I started challenging those *"what if"* scenarios in my head. Like, what if I fail? Okay, sure, but what if I don't? What if it actually works out? And even if it doesn't, what's the worst that could happen? Spoiler alert: it's rarely as bad as we imagine.

Breaking free also means being okay with imperfection. For the longest time, I wouldn't start anything unless I was 100% sure I could crush it. But here's the kicker: waiting for perfection is just another way of staying stuck.

Here's what I want you to take away from this chapter: the mind cage isn't as solid as it seems. The bars are often made of fears and doubts that we've been carrying for years. But the good news? You hold the key.
It starts with recognizing the cage for what it is—just thoughts. And thoughts can be changed. Little by little, challenge them. Push back against the doubts, the fears, and the stories you've been telling yourself. Because on the other side of that cage? That's where freedom lives.

And trust me, it's worth every awkward, messy, imperfect step to get there.

Overcoming Self-Limiting Beliefs

Let's get real for a second: self-limiting beliefs are like that annoying song lyric that gets stuck in your head—you didn't ask for it, but there it is, playing on repeat. For the longest time, I let mine run the show.

I told myself things like, *"I'm just not cut out for this,"* or, *"People like me don't get those kinds of opportunities."* And let's not forget the classic, *"What will everyone think if I mess up?"* Looking back, I can't believe I gave so much power to those thoughts.

Here's how it usually starts: you try something new, it doesn't go perfectly, and suddenly your brain goes, *"See? I told you so. This isn't for you."* But what I've learned is this—self-limiting beliefs are sneaky. They disguise themselves as caution, practicality, or even logic.

For me, the wake-up call came during a presentation I had to give at work. I was convinced I wasn't smart enough to answer tough questions, so I avoided presenting altogether. But when I finally had no choice, something amazing happened—I didn't crash and burn. Were there awkward moments? Sure. But I also realized that the fear of failure was way worse than the actual experience.

That moment sparked something. If I could challenge one belief, what else was I wrong about?
Let me ask you something: have you ever stopped to question the things you believe about yourself? Seriously, think about it. How many of your "I can't" are based on actual evidence versus assumptions you've just accepted over time?

The turning point for me was realizing that beliefs aren't facts. They're just stories we tell ourselves—and the good news is, we can rewrite them.

Start small. Pick one belief that's been holding you back. Maybe it's, *"I'm not good with money,"* or, *"I'm too old to start something new."* Challenge it. Ask yourself, *"Is this really true? Or is it just a story I've been telling myself for so long that it feels true?"*

For example, I used to think, *"I'm not creative."* Then I tried journaling for fun—no pressure, no expectations—and surprise, I actually enjoyed it. Turns out, I wasn't uncreative; I was just too scared to explore it.

Another thing that helped? Surrounding myself with people who see potential in me when I can't see it in myself. A friend once said to me, "You know, your problem isn't that you're not capable. It's that you don't trust yourself to figure it out." That hit like a ton of bricks.

Here's the thing: self-limiting beliefs will always be there, whispering in the background. But the more you challenge them, the quieter they get. It's not about erasing doubt completely—it's about learning to act in spite of it.

So, here's your homework: the next time you hear that little voice saying, *"You can't,"* I want you to answer back with, *"But what if I can?"* Every great thing starts with someone who decides to try, even when they aren't sure they can.

You've got this. And if you don't believe me, borrow a little of my belief in you until you do. Deal?

Stories of Doubt and Breakthrough

Doubt is something we've all felt. It sneaks in when we're trying something new or stepping out of our comfort zone. It's like that little voice in your head that says, *"What if this doesn't work?"* But here's the truth: everyone experiences doubt, no matter how confident they seem.

I remember one of my first big moments of doubt. It was during my first job, and I had to give a presentation in front of a group of experienced professionals. My mind was racing with questions: *"What if I mess up? What if they don't like my idea?"*

I stumbled a little at the beginning, but you know what? The rest of the presentation went just fine. No one criticized me. In fact, someone even said, *"That's a fresh perspective."* That one small comment gave me so much relief.

It took me a while to realize that doubt doesn't just vanish. You have to face it head-on. It's like walking through a dark tunnel—you won't see the light unless you take the first step.

I remember talking about this with a friend who wanted to start his own business but was scared to leave his stable job. He told me, *"What if I fail?"*
I simply asked, *"What if you succeed?"*

That one question changed his perspective. He eventually took the leap, and though it wasn't always smooth, he says it was the best decision he ever made.
Then there was another friend who was terrified of public speaking. She had to give a presentation at work and was dreading it. The night before, she called me, overwhelmed with fear.
I told her, *"Focus on just saying the first sentence. Don't think about the rest yet. One step at a time."*

The next day, she got through it. It wasn't perfect, but she realized she could do it. That small success gave her the confidence to keep improving.

What I've learned is this: breakthroughs don't happen when you wait for the fear to disappear. They happen when you move forward despite the fear.
Doubt is natural. It's part of being human. But it doesn't have to stop you. Start small, take a step, and trust yourself. Even the tiniest step forward can lead to something amazing.

Key Takeaways

1. Overcoming Self-Limiting Beliefs

- This chapter highlights how self-limiting beliefs can hold us back from reaching our full potential.
- Recognizing and challenging these beliefs is crucial in breaking free from mental barriers and unlocking new possibilities.

2. Stories of Doubt and Breakthrough

- Personal stories illustrate how doubt and fear are natural but can be overcome with persistence and self-belief.
- Breakthrough moments often come when we push through our fears and embrace change, showing that growth is possible.

Homework

Write down any self-limiting beliefs you hold about yourself (e.g., *"I'm not good enough," "I'll never succeed").*

- For each belief, challenge it with a counter-affirmation (e.g., *"I am capable of success"*).
- Reflect on a time when you faced doubt but still succeeded, and write down the lessons learned from that experience.

CHAPTER THREE

MASTERING THE PRESENT MOMENT

You know how we often hear phrases like *"Live in the moment"* or *"Be present"*? It sounds simple, but when life gets chaotic, it feels impossible. Our minds are either replaying past mistakes or fast-forwarding to future worries.

I'll be honest, I used to be a pro at overthinking. I'd replay awkward conversations in my head, thinking of better things I could have said. And then, I'd jump ahead to imaginary scenarios about how things might go wrong. I was everywhere except where I needed to be—right here, in the present.

One day, I had an eye-opener. I was sitting with a friend at a café, and he suddenly said, *"You're not even here, are you?"* I blinked, realizing I hadn't heard a single word he'd been saying for the past five minutes. My mind was miles away, worrying about a deadline I had the next week.

He laughed and added, *"Your coffee's gone cold. You should've at least enjoyed that!"*

That moment hit me. I realized I was letting so many moments slip by because I was too focused on things I couldn't control. Mastering the present moment doesn't mean you ignore the past or future—it means you give your full attention to what's happening right now. It's not always easy, but small shifts can make a huge difference.

Here's one thing I started doing: when I feel my mind drifting, I stop and focus on my senses. What do I see? What do I hear? What do I feel? It might sound silly, but it works. It's like grounding yourself in reality.

I also tried something fun with another friend. We decided to go on a hike but left our phones behind. No pictures, no texts, just us and the trail. At first, it felt weird—we're so used to documenting everything. But by the end, it was one of the most refreshing experiences. We laughed about how out of breath we got on steep climbs and how we'd never noticed how beautiful the wildflowers were.

Living in the present doesn't mean you ignore responsibilities or stop planning. It just means you make a conscious effort to be fully engaged in what you're doing now.

So, next time you're sipping coffee, really taste it. When you're talking to someone, truly listen. And if your mind starts to wander, gently pull it back.
The present moment is where life happens. Don't let it slip away unnoticed.

Practical Techniques I Used to Stay Present

After I realized how much of life I was missing by not staying in the moment, I decided to try out some techniques to help me focus. Now, I'm not claiming to be some zen master who never gets distracted (trust me, I'm human). But these small habits have made a big difference for me, and I hope they can for you too.

1. The 5-4-3-2-1 Grounding Technique

This one's my go-to, especially when my mind is racing. It's simple:

- Name 5 things you can see.
- Name 4 things you can feel.
- Name 3 things you can hear.
- Name 2 things you can smell.
- Name 1 thing you can taste.

It's like hitting the reset button on your brain. I once did this during a tense meeting when I started spiraling into *"what-if"* scenarios. I focused on the clicking of the pens, the texture of the chair, the faint smell of coffee, and suddenly, I was back in the room.

2. One-Task-at-a-Time Rule

I used to think multitasking was a superpower. Spoiler alert: it's not. All it did was make me feel scattered and unproductive. Now, I focus on one task at a time. If I'm writing, I'm writing—not checking emails or scrolling through Instagram.
Funny story: I once tried eating lunch while replying to messages. Let's just say spilling soup on my keyboard wasn't exactly productive. That day, I learned the importance of giving each task my undivided attention.

3. Scheduled Daydreaming

This might sound counterintuitive, but setting aside *"daydreaming time"* works wonders. Instead of letting my thoughts wander during important moments, I give myself 10 minutes to think about whatever I want—future plans, silly scenarios, or even imagining what I'd do if I won the lottery. It's like a guilt-free mental vacation.

Small Wins and Big Lessons

At first, I thought staying present was all about huge breakthroughs, like meditating for hours or taking a silent retreat. Turns out, it's the small wins that matter most.

- **Win #1: Enjoying the Little Things**
  There was this one morning I decided to have breakfast on my balcony instead of rushing to my desk. The sunlight felt warm, the coffee tasted better than usual, and the birds sounded like they were putting on a concert just for me. That small act of slowing down changed the tone of my entire day.
- **Win #2: Letting Go of What I Can't Control**
  I used to get stuck on things beyond my control—like traffic or unexpected delays. Once, I was stuck in a massive jam. Normally, I'd stew in frustration, but that day, I turned on a playlist of cheesy 90s songs and sang my heart out. By the time I reached my destination, I was in a surprisingly good mood.
- **Lesson: Progress, Not Perfection**
  I still have moments when my mind drifts or I slip into old habits. And that's okay. What matters is catching myself and coming back. Every time I manage to stay present—even if it's just for a minute—I consider it a win.

It's not about being perfect; it's about trying. These little shifts add up, and before you know it, you'll start noticing the beauty in moments you once overlooked.

So, take it slow. Celebrate the small wins. And remember, staying present isn't about having a perfect day—it's about making the most of the one you're in.

Key Takeaways

1. Practical Techniques I Used to Stay Present

- Staying present is key to overcoming distractions and focusing on what matters.
- Techniques like deep breathing, mindfulness, and grounding exercises help center your attention on the current moment.

2. Small Wins and Big Lessons

- Small wins accumulate over time, leading to big breakthroughs.
- Embracing the present moment allows you to celebrate each small victory, which builds confidence and momentum for larger successes.

Homework

- Try using one of the mindfulness techniques (e.g., deep breathing or focusing on your senses) for 5 minutes each day.
- Reflect on a recent small win and write down how it made you feel and the lessons you learned from it.
- Identify one area where you tend to get distracted and practice staying fully present for 10 minutes each day in that area.

CHAPTER FOUR

DECODING DECISION-MAKING

If there's one thing we all have in common, it's the constant need to make decisions—big ones, small ones, and the *"I can't believe I'm spending 15 minutes deciding what to eat"* ones. Let me tell you, decision-making hasn't always been my strong suit. There were times when I got it all wrong, and times when I somehow got it right. But the key was learning from those experiences.

Let me take you back to a moment that taught me a lot.

A few years ago, I had two job offers on my plate. One was for a position with a fancy title and impressive perks, but the role didn't align with what I really wanted to do. The other was a smaller role in a field I was passionate about but didn't pay as much. Guess which one I picked? The fancy title. Guess how that turned out? Let's just say I spent six months feeling like a fish out of water.

That experience was a turning point. I realized that I'd made my choice based on how it would look to others, not how it felt to me. From then on, I started evaluating decisions differently—focusing on what aligned with my values, not just what seemed impressive.

Lessons Learned from Choices

Looking back, I can't help but smile at some of the decisions I've made—both the brilliant ones and the ones that had me asking, What was I thinking? But here's the thing: every choice taught me something valuable. It's like building a playlist; sometimes you pick the perfect song, and other times you end up skipping halfway through.

Let's dive into a few key lessons I've gathered from my journey through decision-making.

Lesson 1: Clarity Comes from Action

There's a point in life where you realize that overthinking won't give you the clarity you're searching for—only action will. One time, I spent weeks debating whether I should take a part-time course to improve my skills. I'd list the pros, then the cons, then re-list the pros (with slight edits). It was exhausting. Eventually, I just signed up for it. Was it the perfect decision? No. But it helped me discover what I wanted to focus on next.

Takeaway: Sometimes, you've just got to make a move and trust that clarity will follow.

Lesson 2: Impressing Others Is a Terrible Compass

There's a funny thing about choices—we often make them for the approval of others without even realizing it. Like that time I bought an expensive gadget because all my friends were raving about it. Turns out, I barely used it. What I really needed was a simpler tool, but I let the *"cool factor"* sway me.

Takeaway: Focus on what makes sense for you, not what will impress the crowd.

Lesson 3: Mistakes Are Stepping Stones

One of my most important lessons? Mistakes aren't the end of the world—they're the bridge to better decisions. I once accepted a freelance gig purely for the money, even though I knew it wasn't a good fit. A month in, I was burnt out and frustrated. But that mistake taught me to value work-life balance more than a paycheck.

Takeaway: Mistakes are just part of the process. Learn from them and move forward.

Funny Story Time

I remember a time when Amol and I were trying to decide where to eat. We stood outside two restaurants for way too long, debating everything from portion sizes to parking spots. Finally, we flipped a coin and walked into a place known for its *"authentic"* pasta. Let's just say the pasta was so authentic it felt like it skipped the cooking step. Amol joked, *"Next time, we let the parking spot decide."*
Takeaway: Don't let decision fatigue ruin the fun—sometimes, any choice is better than none!

Now It's Your Turn

Think about a choice you've been stuck on recently. What's holding you back? Is it fear, overthinking, or the desire to please others? Write it down, and then ask yourself: What's the worst that could happen if I just go for it?

Remember, every decision—whether it works out or not—is shaping your path. Make it count. And don't worry about choosing the wrong pasta; even that makes for a great story.

Build Confidence in Your Choices

Over time, I learned to trust myself more. The trick is 'Start small'. Test your decision-making on less critical things, like trying a new dish at your favorite restaurant or picking a book without reading the reviews.

Funny story—my friend Amol once dared me to choose a dessert without asking the waiter for recommendations. I ended up with something called *"choco-mystery."* It turned out to be a

surprise mix of chocolate and jalapeños. Did I regret it? A little. Did I learn to live with my choice? Absolutely.
Building confidence isn't about always being right; it's about owning your decisions, even if they don't go perfectly.

Your Turn: Practical Steps to Better Decisions

1. Create a Pro/Con List: Write it out. Seeing the options clearly can be a game-changer.
2. Pause Before You Decide: Take a few deep breaths or sleep on it, if possible.
3. Trust Your Gut: Sometimes, your instincts know more than your overthinking mind.

Decision-making can feel like a daunting task, but every choice you make is a step toward clarity and confidence. And hey, if you end up with a dessert that tastes like spicy chocolate? At least it'll be a story to laugh about later.

Key Takeaways

1. Lessons Learned from Poor and Wise Choices

- Poor decisions often come from fear, lack of information, or ignoring intuition.
- Wise decisions are guided by clarity, careful thought, and trusting your instincts.
- Both poor and wise decisions are learning experiences—embrace them to grow.

2. Building Confidence in Your Decisions

- Confidence comes with practice and trusting yourself.
- Break down big decisions into smaller steps, gather information, and give yourself time to reflect.
- Understand that no decision is ever perfect, but acting confidently leads to progress.

Homework

- Think of a recent poor decision. Write down what you learned from it and how you can avoid it next time.
- Reflect on a decision you made with confidence. What was the outcome? Write about how trusting your judgment affected that decision.
- For a current decision you're facing, break it into smaller steps and practice trusting yourself in each step.

CHAPTER FIVE

Shifting Focus and Priorities

Have you ever been so caught up in chasing something that you forgot why you started in the first place? I've been there more times than I'd like to admit. Shifting focus and priorities isn't easy—it's like trying to reprogram your GPS mid-journey when you're not even sure where the nearest gas station is. But here's the thing: sometimes, taking a detour is the smartest decision you can make.

When Focus Becomes a Blind Spot

For a long time, I thought my focus was my strength. I'd lock onto a goal and sprint toward it like a racehorse with blinders on. But here's the downside: I became so single-minded that I missed out on opportunities and experiences that could have enriched my life.

One time, I was so focused on meeting a professional milestone that I neglected my health. Late nights, skipped meals, and caffeine-fueled mornings were my routine. I finally realized the toll it had taken on me when I couldn't even climb a flight of stairs without feeling winded. It hit me: what good is achieving a goal if you're too burned out to enjoy it?

Prioritizing What Truly Matters

Shifting priorities doesn't mean abandoning your dreams; it means aligning them with what truly matters. For me, that meant redefining success—not as a checklist of accomplishments but as a balance between growth, relationships, and well-being.

I started by taking a hard look at how I was spending my days. I realized that I was giving most of my energy to things that only brought me minimal satisfaction. So, I flipped it. I focused on what genuinely made me feel fulfilled.

I also defined non-negotiables in my life. These were things I refused to compromise on, like dedicating weekends to family and making time for exercise, no matter how busy life got.

I remember telling Amol about my *"new life priorities."* He smirked and said, *"So, does this mean you'll stop obsessing over the perfect Instagram caption?"* (He had a point—I once spent an hour editing a single post!) I laughed and replied, "No promises, but I'll try."

The Art of Saying No

Here's a game-changer: learning to say *"no"* without guilt. I used to agree with everything, thinking it made me reliable. In reality, it just made me overwhelmed. Now, if something doesn't align with my priorities, I politely decline. It's liberating to let go of the fear of disappointing others.

Your Turn

Take a moment to ask yourself if you're focusing on what truly matters. Reflect on whether there's something you need to let go of to make room for what's important. Write down one thing you want to prioritize and one thing you're ready to shift your focus away from.

Life isn't a straight path—it's a winding road with plenty of chances to reroute. And that's a good thing. Sometimes, the best views come from the detours.

Letting Go of Distractions

Distractions. They sneak into our lives like uninvited guests at a party, taking over until you barely remember why you showed up in the first place. For me, letting go of distractions wasn't just about regaining focus; it was about reclaiming my time and energy.

I used to think I was great at multitasking. You know the drill: checking emails while listening to a podcast, scrolling social media while pretending to watch a documentary. It felt productive—until I realized I wasn't actually absorbing anything. My attention was like a toddler running from one shiny toy to another, never settling long enough to truly engage.

One day, my friend caught me during one of my infamous *"productive"* sessions. I was halfway through responding to an email, scrolling Instagram, and jotting down ideas for a project. He looked at me, shook his head, and said, *"You're not multitasking; you're multi-distracting."*

At first, I laughed it off, but later, his words stuck with me. He was right. My brain wasn't switching between tasks; it was scattered, like a browser with too many tabs open. And just like a sluggish computer, I wasn't performing at my best.

Making the Shift

Letting go of distractions wasn't easy. I had to start by identifying them. For me, it was the constant ping of notifications, the endless scroll of social media, and even the urge to check my phone whenever I hit a mental block.

The first thing I did was turn off non-essential notifications. No more buzzing for every like or comment on social media. The world didn't end, and to my surprise, I felt a little lighter without the constant interruptions.

Then came the big one: I started setting specific times for using social media. At first, it felt strange, like I was missing out on something. But over time, I realized how much mental clarity I gained when I wasn't hopping between tasks.

My friend found it hilarious when I told him about my *"phone detox"* plan. He said, *"Let me guess—next, you'll move to the mountains and meditate with monks?"* I replied, *"Not quite, but I might finally finish a book without checking my phone every five minutes!"*

So, the Bigger Picture is *'Letting go of distractions'* isn't just about improving productivity. It's about being present in your own life. I started noticing little things I'd been overlooking—like how good it felt to have a real conversation without glancing at my phone or how much I enjoyed walking outside without headphones on.

Distractions rob us of these simple, meaningful moments. Letting go of them is like clearing the clutter from a room—you make space for what truly matters.

How I Realigned My Life with My Values

Realigning my life with my values wasn't something that happened overnight. It was more like trying to untangle a mess of earphone wires—you know there's a starting point somewhere, but it takes patience to figure it out.

There was a point when I felt like I was on autopilot. I was busy, yes, but was I fulfilled? Not really. It hit me one evening when I sat down, exhausted after another packed day of meetings and tasks. I had this moment of clarity: I was doing a lot, but not necessarily the right things. My life felt like it was full, yet hollow.

That's when I started thinking about my values. What truly mattered to me? Was it just about meeting deadlines and ticking off to-do lists, or was there something deeper I was missing?

I remember having a conversation with my younger brother during this phase. He asked me, *"What's one thing you'd regret not doing if today was your last day?"* I laughed at first—typical of my brother, always dramatic. But then I couldn't stop thinking about it. My answer surprised me. It wasn't about career achievements or financial milestones. It was about relationships, growth, and the sense of contributing something meaningful to the world.

From that day, I started by listing out the things I genuinely valued. Family came first, followed by personal growth, creativity, and helping others. It sounds simple, but when I compared that list to how I was actually spending my time, there was a glaring mismatch.

For example, I valued family, but I was constantly *"too busy"* to sit down for dinner with them. I valued personal growth, but most of my free time went into mindless scrolling rather than reading or learning. Realigning meant making conscious choices to prioritize these values, even when it wasn't convenient.

One small change I made was setting aside tech-free time in the evenings. At first, it was awkward. I'd find myself reaching for my phone out of habit. But then I started noticing things I'd been missing—like how my mom always hums while cooking or how my dad tells the same jokes but laughs at them like they're brand new.

My brother once caught me reading a book on mindfulness. He smirked and said, "Oh, so now you're all about inner peace? Next, you'll be meditating on mountaintops!" I replied, "Not yet, but I might be able to sit through a meeting without zoning out."

The Payoff

Realigning my life with my values didn't mean making huge sacrifices. It was more about small, consistent changes that brought me closer to what truly mattered. And the funny thing?

The more I focused on these core values, the less drained I felt. Life started feeling lighter, and more purposeful.

If you're feeling off track, take a moment to think about your own values. What matters most to you? Are your actions aligned with those priorities? It's not always an easy process, but trust me, the clarity and peace you gain are worth every bit of effort.

And remember, it's okay to laugh at yourself along the way. Life's too short to take everything too seriously—even realigning with your values.

Key Takeaways

1. Letting Go of Distractions

- Distractions often stem from trying to please others or chasing unimportant goals.
- Identify what truly matters in your life and eliminate time-wasters.
- Practice saying *"no"* to things that don't align with your values or long-term goals.

2. How I Realigned My Life with My Values

- Understanding your core values helps you prioritize what's important.
- Realignment involves making choices that reflect your true self, not just external expectations.
- Regular self-reflection ensures you stay aligned with your values and continue growing.

Homework

- Identify 3 major distractions in your life. Write down how you can eliminate or minimize them.
- Reflect on your top 3 values. How do they influence your daily decisions? Write down one change you can make today to realign your actions with those values.

CHAPTER SIX

Embracing Challenges as Opportunities

Challenges have a way of showing up when you least expect them. It's like they sit in a corner, waiting for the perfect moment to pounce—usually when you're already juggling ten other things. For the longest time, I saw challenges as roadblocks, something to grit my teeth and power through. But over time, I realized they could be much more than that.

Let me tell you about one of the toughest moments I faced. It was a project at work that felt impossible—tight deadlines, unclear goals, and a team that wasn't exactly motivated. At first, I did what most of us do: I panicked. Then I complained. And then I panicked some more.

It wasn't until I took a step back that I saw the situation differently. Instead of focusing on everything that could go wrong, I asked myself, *"What can I learn from this? How can I use this mess to grow?"* That shift in mindset didn't magically solve the problems, but it gave me the energy and creativity to tackle them differently.

My friend once told me, *"Challenges are just opportunities in ugly disguises."* I shot back, "Well, this opportunity is wearing the worst disguise ever. It's like a monster costume from a bad horror movie!" We laughed, but there was truth in what he said. Challenges do come disguised, and they rarely look like something you'd willingly embrace.

If you ask me what changed for me, so I started seeing challenges as opportunities to stretch myself. Every tough situation became a chance to test my patience, improve my skills, or simply prove to myself that I could handle more than I thought. For example, that work project? It forced me to learn how to communicate better with my team, set clearer priorities, and stay calm under pressure. These were lessons I wouldn't have picked up if everything had gone smoothly.

A Personal Breakthrough

One of the biggest challenges I faced was public speaking. Just the thought of standing in front of an audience made me want to disappear. But when I was asked to give a presentation, I couldn't say no. I was terrified, but I knew it was an opportunity to face a fear that had been holding me back for years.I'll admit, the first few minutes were rough. My voice cracked, my hands shook, and I stumbled over my words. But then something amazing happened. As I kept going, I realized the audience wasn't judging me—they were rooting for me. That moment taught me that challenges aren't just obstacles; they're mirrors that show you what you're capable of.

Now, when a challenge comes my way, I ask myself, "How can this make me better?" It's not about being overly optimistic or pretending everything is great. It's about finding value in the struggle. And sometimes, the value is simply realizing that you're stronger than you think.

So, the next time life throws a curveball your way, take a deep breath and ask yourself: What can this teach me? And if it feels like too much, remember that even the toughest moments eventually pass. Who knows? You might look back one day and realize that what felt like a setback was actually a step forward.

And if nothing else, you'll at least have a good story to laugh about later. For example, I tried to cook for a group of friends to prove I could handle pressure, and I ended up serving charred pasta. It turns out that not every challenge leads to success, but all challenges lead to growth.

Personal Stories of Turning Setbacks into Stepping Stones

There's a saying I love: *"Every setback is a setup for a comeback."* It sounds great in theory, right? But when life throws you a curveball, it's hard to see it that way. I learned this lesson the hard way during one of the most frustrating phases of my life.

It started with a project I was ridiculously excited about. I had poured my heart into this idea for months, mapping every detail, and imagining how it would all unfold. I even told a few close friends about it, convinced it was going to be a game-changer. And then, just as things were picking up, everything fell apart.

The main investor backed out. A couple of key people I was relying on decided they couldn't commit. Suddenly, what felt like a sure thing turned into a giant question mark. I remember sitting in my room that night, staring at my laptop, wondering if I'd just wasted months of effort.

I won't lie—it stung. It stung badly. But here's the thing: after the initial wave of frustration, I decided to look at what had gone wrong. I had been so focused on the big idea that I hadn't paid enough attention to the smaller but critical details. I realized that setbacks like these weren't just failures; they were feedback.

Here's where it gets interesting. That failed project? It forced me to rethink my approach. Instead of giving up, I started breaking things down into smaller, manageable parts. I revisited the idea with a sharper focus, found better collaborators, and pitched it again with more clarity. Guess what? It worked the second time. And honestly, it turned out much better than my original plan ever could have been.

I remember sharing this story with my friend once over chai. He laughed and said, *"So, failure is like that one annoying friend who keeps giving you unsolicited advice, huh?"* I laughed and nodded. That's exactly what it felt like—annoying but, in the end, helpful.

Another story that sticks with me is from my college days. I had completely bombed an important exam. You know that sinking feeling when you walk out of the exam hall and just know you've messed up? Yeah, that was me. For weeks, I beat myself up over it, convinced I wasn't good enough. But then something unexpected happened.

One of my professors called me in and said, *"You're looking at this the wrong way. You're so focused on this one result that you're ignoring everything else you've done well."* That conversation shifted something in me. I stopped seeing the failure as a reflection of who I was and started treating it as a learning moment.
It wasn't easy, but I worked harder, sought help when I needed it, and made adjustments to my study habits. By the end of that semester, not only had I passed, but I had aced the subject that had initially tripped me up. That setback had become my stepping stone.

Looking back, these experiences taught me a simple truth: setbacks are inevitable, but they don't define you. What defines you is how you choose to respond. You can let them break you, or you can use them to build something better.

And let's not forget—they make for great stories later. Like the time I accidentally submitted the wrong file for a client presentation and had to improvise the whole thing on the spot. It was a disaster at the time, but now it's one of those stories I tell to remind myself that even the worst moments have a way of turning into something valuable.

Strategies for Building Resilience

Resilience is a word we hear often, but what does it really mean? For me, it's like being a rubber band. Life stretches you, sometimes to your limits, but resilience is what helps you bounce back instead of snapping. But here's the catch: it's not something you're born with—it's something you build, little by little, like a skill.

I remember when I first realized the importance of resilience. It was during a phase when everything seemed to be going wrong. Work was a mess, personal life felt chaotic, and I couldn't catch a break. One evening, a friend and I went for a walk to clear our heads. Out of nowhere, he said, *"You know, we're like that old scooter in my garage. It's been through storms, bumps, and breakdowns, but it still runs when I need it most."*

At first, I laughed. Comparing ourselves to a rusty scooter wasn't exactly inspiring. But then it hit me: resilience doesn't mean you're perfect or unbreakable. It means you keep going, even when you've been through the wringer.

So, how do you build resilience? For me, it started with small steps. One thing I learned was to focus on what I could control. There was a time when I let little things—traffic jams, delayed emails, or minor mistakes—completely derail my day. Now, when something like that happens, I take a deep breath and ask myself, *"Will this matter a week from now?"* Spoiler: it rarely does.

Another thing that helped was reframing my mindset. Instead of seeing challenges as obstacles, I started seeing them as opportunities to grow. That doesn't mean I was thrilled about every setback. Far from it. But I realized that every time life knocked me down, I came back a little stronger, a little smarter.

One funny story comes to mind. I once had to give a big presentation, and I spent weeks preparing for it. On the day of the event, the projector failed, my slides wouldn't load, and I had to wing it with just a whiteboard and a marker. I was mortified at first, but the audience loved it. They said it felt more personal and engaging than a typical slide deck. That day, I learned that resilience also means being adaptable—rolling with the punches instead of freezing up.

And let's not forget the power of humor. When life gets too heavy, a good laugh can lighten the load. I have a friend who, no matter how bad things get, always cracks a joke. One time, after a particularly tough day, he said, *"Hey, at least we're not stuck in a Bollywood soap opera where everyone's crying all the time."* That one line made me laugh so hard, I forgot why I was upset in the first place.

Lastly, I've realized that resilience isn't a solo journey. Surrounding yourself with supportive people—friends, family, mentors—can make all the difference. They remind you of your strength when you forget it yourself.

Building resilience doesn't happen overnight, but every small step counts. It's in the little things: choosing to get back up after a fall, finding a silver lining in a storm, or even just having faith that tomorrow is another chance to try again. So, the next time life stretches you, remember: you're that rubber band. You're tougher than you think.

Key Takeaways

1. Personal Stories of Turning Setbacks into Stepping Stones

- Challenges and setbacks can be transformed into valuable learning experiences.
- Reframe failures as opportunities for growth and a chance to build stronger resilience.
- Every obstacle faced has the potential to shape you into a better version of yourself.

2. Strategies for Building Resilience

- Stay connected with a supportive network of people who encourage and motivate you.
- Focus on developing a positive mindset to overcome difficulties with a solution-oriented approach.
- Build emotional flexibility by learning to adapt to change and bouncing back from setbacks.

Homework

- Write about a recent challenge you faced. How can you view it as a stepping stone toward your growth?
- Identify one strategy you can start implementing today to build resilience, such as journaling, meditation, or seeking support from someone you trust

CHAPTER SEVEN

The Power of Daily Habits

Daily habits are like the unsung heroes of our lives. They're the small, seemingly insignificant actions that, over time, shape who we are and where we're headed. Think about it—brushing your teeth doesn't give you sparkling results overnight, but skipping it for a month? Well, let's not even go there.

I used to underestimate the power of daily habits. I thought big goals needed big leaps, not tiny steps. But one day, during a conversation with an old friend, something clicked. He was telling me how he had started learning guitar. *"Five minutes a day,"* he said casually. I laughed. *"Five minutes? That's barely enough to tune the thing!"* He shrugged. *"Yeah, but I've been at it for six months now, and I can actually play a few songs."*

That got me thinking. It wasn't about how much time he spent each day; it was the consistency. Small efforts, repeated daily, were adding up to something big.

So, I decided to experiment. I picked one habit—waking up 30 minutes earlier than usual. The first few days were rough. Let's just say I had a strong love-hate relationship with my snooze button. But after a week, I started enjoying the quiet mornings. I'd sip my tea, plan my day, and sometimes just sit and breathe.

It was such a simple change, but it made a huge difference in how I felt. There was this one funny incident during those early wake-up days. I had told a friend about my *"new life as a morning person."* One evening, he called me at 11 PM and said, *"Hey, let's see a late-night movie. You're cool, right?"* Without thinking, I said yes. The next morning, my alarm rang, and I stared at it like it had betrayed me. But I dragged myself out of bed anyway. That day, I realized the importance of setting boundaries to protect your habits.

Habits also taught me patience. I wanted instant results—who doesn't? But life doesn't work that way. When I started journaling every night, I thought I'd have profound revelations within a week. Spoiler alert: most entries were about how tired I felt or what I ate for lunch. But over time, patterns emerged. I began to notice what made me happy, what drained me, and what I needed to change.

One of the best lessons I've learned is that habits don't have to be perfect to be powerful. Missing a day or slipping up doesn't mean you've failed. It just means you're human. The trick is to get back on track without beating yourself up.

Let's not forget how habits stack up over time. I call it the *"snowball effect."* You start small—reading one page of a book, drinking an extra glass of water, or taking a five-minute walk. Soon, these small actions lead to bigger changes. Before you know it, you're finishing books, feeling healthier, and maybe even signing up for a marathon (okay, maybe not a marathon, but you get the idea).

Try it today:

If you've ever doubted the power of daily habits, try this: pick one tiny habit and stick to it for a month. It could be as simple as making your bed or writing down one thing you're grateful for each day. I promise, by the end of the month, you'll feel a subtle but profound shift.

Habits are like planting seeds. At first, it feels like nothing's happening. But with time and care, those seeds grow into something beautiful—something you might not have even imagined.

How I Designed My Daily Routine

Designing my daily routine was like piecing together a jigsaw puzzle, except I didn't have the picture on the box to guide me. It wasn't about creating the *"perfect"* day but about finding what worked for me—something realistic and sustainable. And let me tell you, the process was far from flawless, but it was full of funny moments and a lot of trial and error.

It all started when I noticed how chaotic my days felt. I'd wake up late, rush through my mornings, and spend the rest of the day playing catch-up. By evening, I was too exhausted to do anything meaningful, and the cycle would repeat. One evening, while scrolling through my phone and munching on snacks, I thought, What if I just made a plan and stuck to it for once?

The first draft of my routine was overly ambitious—workout at 6 AM, meditate, journal, prepare a gourmet breakfast, and start work by 8 AM. It sounded like something out of a productivity guru's playbook. The first day, I skipped the workout, turned meditation into a nap, and ate cereal straight from the box. It was clear I needed a more realistic approach.

So, I stripped it down to the basics. I picked three priorities: wake up earlier, exercise for ten minutes, and plan my day over coffee. Nothing fancy, but manageable.

One morning, while I was doing a clumsy version of yoga in my living room, my friend called. *"Are you okay?"* he asked, hearing my heavy breathing. I told him I was trying to follow a YouTube yoga tutorial. *"Does it involve wrestling a bear?"* he joked. That laugh reminded me not to take myself too seriously.
The real magic happened when I started building flexibility into my routine. Some days, I felt like going for a walk instead of doing yoga. On other days, my *"planning session"* was just a quick mental checklist while sipping tea. And you know what? That was

fine. The key was consistency, not perfection.

One habit that really stuck was starting my mornings without my phone. No scrolling, no notifications. At first, it was hard. My phone practically called to me, and I'd catch myself reaching for it automatically. But after a few weeks, I realized how much more peaceful my mornings felt without it.

Designing a routine also meant understanding my energy levels throughout the day. I noticed I was most productive in the mornings and hit a slump in the afternoons. Instead of fighting it, I started scheduling important tasks for the morning and reserving the afternoon for easier, less demanding work.

There were also times when my routine went out the window—like when I stayed up too late watching a series or got caught up in impromptu plans with friends. But instead of feeling guilty, I'd just restart the next day.

Creating my daily routine taught me two important things. First, it's okay to start small. You don't need to overhaul your entire life overnight. Second, your routine should work for you, not the other way around. It's about building a framework that supports your goals and makes your days feel more intentional, not rigid schedules that stress you out.

If you're thinking about designing your own routine, my advice is simple: start with one or two changes and give yourself time to adjust. Experiment, tweak, and don't be afraid to laugh at yourself along the way. After all, life isn't meant to be a checklist; it's meant to be lived.

Small Changes That Made a Big Difference

It's funny how the smallest changes can sometimes have the biggest impact. At first, I didn't believe it. I thought making a difference in life required some grand gesture or a complete lifestyle overhaul. But over time, I realized it's those tiny, almost invisible shifts that pave the way for bigger transformations.

Take drinking water, for instance. I used to forget about it entirely, running on caffeine like a questionable science experiment. One day, my friend casually said, *"You look dehydrated—like a raisin."* I laughed it off but decided to keep a water bottle with me, refilling it throughout the day. It wasn't revolutionary, but suddenly I had more energy, my headaches went away, and, well, I stopped looking like a raisin.

Another small change was swapping out the endless *"to-do lists"* for a simple rule: tackle one important thing first. I'd been that person who wrote ten things down, did two, and felt like a failure by the end of the day. So, I flipped the script. Each morning, I asked myself, *"What's the one thing I absolutely need to do today?"* Focusing on just one task gave me momentum, and funnily enough, I ended up completing more than I used to.

Then there was the time I changed how I used my phone. My screen time was ridiculous, so I tried setting it to grayscale. It was like taking the candy out of a kid's hand—suddenly, Instagram didn't seem so appealing. I still used my phone, but now with more intention, not as an escape. My friend teased me, saying, *"What's next, going back to a Nokia 3310?"* Maybe someday, who knows?

Small adjustments to my mornings also made a difference. Instead of snoozing my alarm three times (okay, five), I moved my alarm clock to the other side of the room. This meant I had to physically get up to turn it off. It was annoying but effective. Waking up earlier gave me a few precious minutes of calm before the chaos of the day began.

I also stopped multitasking. At first, it felt strange to just do one thing at a time—like eating without scrolling or working without jumping between tabs. However, I noticed I felt less stressed and got things done faster. It was like my brain could finally breathe. A friend once joked, *"Are you okay? You're just sitting there, eating like a normal person."* And honestly? It felt great.

Even small shifts in perspective helped. I started celebrating tiny wins—like finishing a book, choosing a healthy snack, or even just getting through a tough day. These small victories added up, making me feel more accomplished and motivated.

The funny thing about these changes is that they seem so minor, they almost feel like cheating. But they worked because they were easy to stick with. I didn't have to rearrange my entire life; I just had to make a few tweaks and stay consistent.

Looking back, I realized the secret wasn't about doing more but doing small things better. Those little shifts became habits, and those habits built the foundation for bigger improvements. It's proof that sometimes, the simplest things can lead to the most surprising outcomes. And hey, if I can do it, anyone can. Even you, raisin or not.

Key Takeaways

1. How I Designed My Daily Routine

- Creating a consistent routine helped me stay focused and productive.
- I prioritized key activities such as exercise, work, and personal time to balance different areas of life.
- The key to success is not in drastic changes, but in building habits that are easy to sustain and that align with your goals.

2. Small Changes That Made a Big Difference

- Small, simple changes, like adjusting my sleep schedule or adding a quick morning workout, had a huge impact on my energy and productivity.
- Regular habits, even tiny ones, compound over time to produce significant results.
- Focusing on consistency rather than perfection was key to making lasting changes.

Homework

- Design your own daily routine, focusing on small, manageable activities that align with your goals.
- Identify one small habit you can implement today that will improve your routine and track its impact for a week.

Cultivating a Growth Mindset

Have you ever felt stuck, like no matter what you do, things just won't change? That was me not so long ago. I'd hear about this *"growth mindset"* thing, and honestly, I thought it was just another buzzword. But then, life threw me a curveball that forced me to rethink everything.

It started with a mistake—one of those big, embarrassing ones. I botched an important project at work, and for days, all I could think about was how I'd failed. A friend called me out, though. *"You know, you're not the only person in history to mess up,"* he said, smirking. *"Stop acting like the world's ending."*

At first, I wanted to snap back, but then it hit me. What if failure wasn't the end of the world? What if it was just... part of the process? That thought opened a door I didn't even know was there. I started reading about the difference between a fixed mindset—where you believe your abilities are set in stone—and a growth mindset, which sees everything as a chance to learn.

The idea was simple but powerful. If I could approach setbacks as lessons instead of final judgments, I could grow from them. So, I tried it. The next time I made a mistake, instead of beating myself up, I asked, *"What went wrong, and what can I do differently next time?"* It wasn't easy, but little by little, I started to see progress.

One of the funniest moments during this shift was when I tried learning a new skill: cooking. Now, anyone who knows me knows that my kitchen skills were limited to boiling water (and even that was questionable). The first time I attempted to make pasta from scratch, it ended in disaster. My dough was so tough, my friend joked, *"You making pasta or building a house?"*

Instead of quitting, I laughed it off and gave it another shot. By the third attempt, I had something edible—and by the fifth,

I had something I was proud to serve. It was a small victory, but it proved a big point: effort and persistence really do make a difference.

This growth mindset thing started spilling into other areas of my life too. Instead of avoiding challenges, I began welcoming them as opportunities to learn. Even the word *"failure"* started feeling less intimidating and more like a stepping stone. My friend once said, *"You're weirdly chill about messing up now."* And honestly, it's been liberating.

One thing I've learned is that cultivating a growth mindset isn't about flipping a switch—it's a process. It's about catching yourself when you fall into old habits of self-doubt and gently reminding yourself, *"This is just a chance to grow."* Some days are easier than others, but every time I lean into this mindset, I feel a little stronger, a little braver.

So, if you're feeling stuck, maybe it's time to start looking at challenges differently. Instead of asking, *"Why me?"* try asking, *"What can I learn from this?"* It's not magic—it's just a small shift in thinking that can lead to big changes. And hey, if I can go from ruining pasta to loving the learning process, you can too. Just don't ask me to bake. That's still a work in progress.

Overcoming Fear of Failure

You know, fear of failure is like that nosy neighbor who keeps peeking through the curtains. Always there, always judging, even when you're just trying to do your thing. I've had my fair share of run-ins with it. And let me tell you, it's sneaky. It doesn't just pop up when you're doing something big and bold. Sometimes, it shows up when you're about to take the smallest step forward, whispering, *"What if this goes wrong?"*

I remember this one time when I had to give a presentation at work. It wasn't even a big deal—just a quick update on a project. But I spent days obsessing over every slide, every word. The night before, I texted a friend, *"What if I completely bomb tomorrow?"* He replied, *"Then you'll become a legendary meme in the office. Aim for fame!"* I laughed, but honestly, the fear was real.

The next day, I messed up my opening line—twice. My voice cracked like I'd just hit puberty all over again, and someone at the back actually chuckled. But then, something surprising happened. Instead of spiraling, I made a joke about it: *"Well, that's one way to break the ice!"* And just like that, the tension melted away. I didn't deliver a perfect presentation, but it was good enough. More importantly, I survived.

That's the thing about fear of failure—it always feels worse in your head than it actually turns out to be. It convinces you that one mistake will ruin everything, when in reality, people are more forgiving than we think. In fact, sometimes your missteps make you more relatable. After all, who doesn't mess up?

Another time, my friend and I decided to try rock climbing. Now, I am not a natural athlete. Heights? Not my thing. But my friend, who was already halfway up the wall, yelled down, *"What's the worst that could happen? You fall? The harness will catch you!"* Easy for him to say while hanging on like Spider-Man. But his point stuck with me. The fear wasn't about the actual fall—it was about how I'd feel if I couldn't do it. Once I realized that, I took a deep breath and went for it. Spoiler alert: I didn't make it to the top. But I got further than I expected, and that felt like a win.

What I've learned is that fear of failure isn't something you overcome in one dramatic moment. It's about taking small steps to face it, proving to yourself over and over that even if you fall, you'll get back up. Sometimes, it's as simple as asking, "What's the worst that could really happen?" When you realize it's not the end of the world, the fear starts to shrink.

So, the next time fear tries to stop you, imagine it as that nosy neighbor. Smile, wave, and keep doing your thing. Let it watch while you climb, stumble, and grow. Because trust me, every step forward—no matter how wobbly—is worth it.

Celebrating Progress over perfection

Celebrating progress over perfection has been a game-changer for me. I used to be one of those people who thought, *"If it's not perfect, why bother?"* It sounds noble, but it's actually exhausting. Perfection is like a treadmill—you keep running, but you never really get anywhere. Progress, though? That's stepping off the treadmill and actually walking forward.

Let me tell you about a silly moment that taught me this lesson. A few years ago, I decided to learn guitar. I had this grand vision of playing soulful songs around a campfire, friends swaying and singing along. In reality, my first attempt at playing sounded like a cat in distress. My friend, who was sitting nearby, couldn't stop laughing. *"What song is that? The anthem of broken strings?"* he teased.

For a moment, I wanted to quit. But then I realized something—I'd managed to play something. It wasn't good, but it was better than nothing. I practiced a little every day, and soon enough, I could fumble through a basic song. Did I sound like a rock star? Absolutely not. But the first time I played something recognizable, it felt like a victory. My friend even said, *"Hey, that didn't make my ears bleed. Progress!"*

This approach spilled over into other parts of my life. When I started working out, I stopped obsessing over achieving the *"perfect"* body. Instead, I celebrated being able to do one extra push-up or run an extra minute without collapsing. At work, I learned to submit drafts that weren't flawless but were a step in the right direction. Every little bit added up.

The problem with chasing perfection is that it makes you blind to how far you've come. I once spent hours editing an article, obsessing over every word. My friend, a writer himself, looked at me and said, *"You know, 90% good is still an A, right?"* That hit me. Sometimes, the extra effort to make something perfect doesn't change the outcome—it just delays it.

Celebrating progress isn't just about being kinder to yourself; it's also more fun. My friends and I started this silly tradition of clinking our coffee mugs whenever one of us hit a small milestone, like finishing a task early or managing not to kill a houseplant for a month. It became this inside joke: *"Cheers to not sucking today!"*

What I've realized is that progress, no matter how small, is worth celebrating. It's those little wins that build momentum and keep you going. The next time you're tempted to hold out for perfection, ask yourself, *"What have I already achieved?"* Even if it's tiny, give yourself a moment to smile about it. And if you have a friend nearby, clink your mugs or make a joke about your progress. It's a lot more satisfying than chasing something that might never come.

Key Takeaways

1. Overcoming Fear of Failure

- Fear of failure is a natural part of growth but should not stop you from taking action.
- Embrace mistakes as learning opportunities, and use them as stepping stones towards your success.
- The more you face challenges, the more resilient and capable you become.

2. Celebrating Progress Over Perfection

- Focus on progress, not perfection. Small steps forward are more important than waiting for the "perfect" moment or outcome.
- Celebrate your achievements, no matter how small, to build confidence and momentum.
- Perfection is a myth—embracing imperfection allows for greater learning and growth.

Homework

Identify one fear or failure you've been avoiding and take a small step toward overcoming it today.

Reflect on one recent achievement, no matter how small, and celebrate it as a sign of progress.

YOUR NETWORK SHAPES YOUR NOW

You know that old saying, *"You're the average of the five people you spend the most time with"?* Well, it turns out, it's painfully true. I didn't believe it at first. I thought, *"Nah, I'm my own person. Nobody can influence me."* But then I started noticing how much my habits, thoughts, and even my energy mirrored the people around me.

Take my friend Rohan, for example. This guy is the definition of laid-back. He can turn a crisis into a comedy skit. Once, we were late for a train, and instead of panicking, he grabbed some chai and said, *"If we miss it, we'll take the next one. Stress is overrated."* I laughed it off at the time, but that moment stuck with me. His calmness started rubbing off on me, and suddenly, I wasn't sweating the small stuff anymore.

On the flip side, I had a phase where I was constantly around people who loved to complain. The weather, their jobs, the neighbor's dog—everything was a problem. I didn't even realize it, but their negativity started seeping into me. One day, I caught myself whining about a slow Wi-Fi connection, and I thought, *"Wait, when did I become this person?"* That's when it hit me: the people you surround yourself with have a huge impact on how you think and act.

So, I started paying attention. I didn't ghost anyone—I mean, who am I, a magician? But I did make a conscious effort to spend more time with people who inspired me. There's Aisha, who's always bursting with creative ideas, and Vikram, who's like a walking TED Talk on productivity. Being around them made me want to up my game, too.

The funny thing is, you don't even need to personally know everyone in your "network." For a while, my biggest influencers were authors and podcasters. I'd listen to their insights and feel like I was part of a conversation with some really smart, motivated people.

One of the coolest moments happened recently when my friend group decided to try something new. Instead of our usual Friday-night banter, we turned it into a *"future swap."* Each of us shared a small goal we were working on, and the rest of the group pitched in ideas to help. It was hilarious, too—one guy wanted to learn salsa dancing, and we spent 20 minutes trying (and failing) to teach him some moves right there in the living room. But the energy? It was electric.

Here's the thing: you don't have to cut ties with everyone who doesn't *"fit"* your goals. It's not about creating some elite club. It's about being mindful of whose energy you absorb the most. Are they pushing you forward or holding you back?

Your network is like your garden. If you water the right connections, they'll grow into something beautiful. And if you accidentally let in a few weeds, it's okay. Just make sure you're still planting enough flowers.

So, who's in your circle? And more importantly, are they helping you shape your "now" into something you're proud of? If not, maybe it's time to mix things up a bit.

Insights from My Relationships and Collaborations

Do you know how every relationship teaches you something? Whether it's a friend, a colleague, or even that one neighbor who always *"borrows"* your newspaper but never returns it—each connection leaves a mark. Some are life lessons, others are just funny stories, but they all shape how you see the world and yourself.

I once worked on a project with a team that could only be described as diverse. There was Karen, who had a spreadsheet for everything, including our coffee breaks. Then there was Rahul, who was the king of big ideas but couldn't meet a deadline to save his life. And let's not forget Mira, the peacemaker who'd bring cookies whenever things got tense.

Initially, it felt like chaos. Karen would get frustrated when Rahul winged presentations. Rahul would roll his eyes at Karen's endless data. Mira and I spent half our time mediating. But as the weeks went by, something magical happened. We started playing to each other's strengths. Karen's data backed up Rahul's wild ideas, giving them credibility. Rahul's energy kept the team motivated when things got tough. Mira's cookies... well, they worked wonders too.

By the end of the project, not only had we created something amazing, but we'd also learned how to appreciate what each person brought to the table. I'll admit, I used to get annoyed when people didn't work the way I did. But this experience taught me that collaboration isn't about everyone being the same—it's about bringing different pieces together to complete the puzzle.

Relationships outside work have been equally eye-opening. Take my old college roommate, Arjun. He was the kind of guy who could turn a five-minute trip to the grocery store into a two-hour adventure because he'd strike up conversations with strangers about everything from politics to the best brand of peanut butter. I used to tease him about it, saying, *"Do you get loyalty points for making friends?"* But you know what? Watching him taught me the value of genuine connection.

Arjun had this knack for making people feel seen, like they mattered. It wasn't about getting something out of it—it was just who he was. And when I started applying that to my own interactions, everything changed. Conversations became deeper, collaborations smoother, and even disagreements felt more productive.

There was also this time I messed up big in a collaboration. I forgot to communicate a key update, and it threw off the entire timeline. Naturally, the team was upset. I braced myself for an avalanche of blame, but instead, my colleague Priya said, *"Hey, we've all been there. Let's fix it and move forward."*

That moment stuck with me. It reminded me how important it is to create a safe space for mistakes. When people feel supported, they're more willing to take risks and think creatively. It's something I try to carry forward in all my relationships now.

Funny thing is, we often think of relationships and collaborations as separate things. But they're not, really. Whether it's a brainstorming session or a heart-to-heart over coffee, the core is the same: understanding, patience, and a little bit of humor.

Like my friend Tasha says, *"Life is messy, but at least we can laugh about it together."* And she's right. Whether it's a project that feels like it's held together by duct tape or a friendship that survives because of inside jokes, the mess is where the magic happens.

So here's what I've learned: Relationships and collaborations are like mirrors. They reflect who we are, challenge us to grow, and sometimes, they just make us laugh. And honestly? That's the best kind of learning.

Building a Support System

Let me ask you something. Have you ever had a day where everything feels like it's falling apart, and then one random text from a friend makes you feel like, *"Okay, maybe I've got this"*? That's the magic of a good support system. It's not just about having people around—it's about having the right people around.

I used to think I could handle everything on my own. You know, the *"lone wolf"* mentality—head down, hustle hard, figure it all out myself. Spoiler alert: it didn't work. One night, after a particularly tough week, I was venting to my friend Riya. She listened patiently, then said, *"You know, it's okay to ask for help. Even superheroes need sidekicks."*

That hit me. Riya wasn't wrong. Batman had Robin. Sherlock had Watson. Even Harry Potter needed Hermione to do all the actual thinking.

So, I started paying attention to who was in my corner. It wasn't about having the biggest group of friends or the most impressive LinkedIn connections. It was about finding people who genuinely cared, who could offer a mix of support, advice, and, when needed, a reality check.

One of the first things I learned? Your support system doesn't have to look a certain way. It could be your best friend from school, your yoga instructor who always has the best life advice, or even your colleague who knows how to navigate office politics like a pro.

For me, it's a mix. My dad is my go-to when I need practical, no-nonsense advice. He'll say things like, *"If you don't fix the roof when the sun is shining, don't complain when it rains."* (Classic Dad wisdom, right?) My best friend, Neha, is my therapist-in-disguise. She's the one who lets me ugly cry on her couch and then makes me laugh with the worst jokes imaginable. And then there's Arjun—remember him? My peanut-butter-debate roommate. He's the one I call when I need someone to talk me out of impulsive decisions, like adopting a second dog because the first one *"needs a friend."*

But here's the thing about building a support system: it's not just about what others can do for you. It's about being that person for them too. When Neha was going through a rough patch last year, I showed up with snacks, a playlist of her favorite songs, and an endless supply of bad puns. (Okay, the puns were mostly for my amusement.)

One of the best lessons I've learned is that a support system thrives on reciprocity. It's not about keeping score—*"I did this for you, so you owe me"*—but about showing up for each other because you want to.

And let's not forget the funny side of things. At that time Amol and I decided to *"support"* each other by starting a fitness routine. On day one, we went for a jog. By day two, we'd turned it into a walking club that ended at the nearest ice cream parlor. We still laugh about it, but honestly? Even those moments built a sense of connection and trust.

A good support system isn't perfect. There will be disagreements, missed calls, and times when someone doesn't know how to help. That's okay. The point is to have people who are there for the long haul—through the highs, the lows, and the ice-cream-detour kind of days.

So, here's my take: building a support system is less about finding people who'll solve your problems and more about surrounding yourself with those who make life's challenges feel a little less daunting. And sometimes, it's just about having someone who'll sit with you in the mess, sharing a tub of ice cream, reminding you that you're not alone.

Key Takeaways

1. Insights from My Relationships and Collaborations

- Your relationships and collaborations significantly impact your growth and success.
- Surrounding yourself with like-minded people who support and challenge you can accelerate your progress.
- Working with others opens doors to new opportunities, ideas, and experiences.

2. Building a Support System

- A strong support system is essential for navigating challenges and staying motivated.
- Surround yourself with people who encourage your dreams, provide honest feedback, and help you stay accountable.
- Invest in relationships that add value to your life and contribute to your personal and professional growth.

Homework

- Reach out to one person in your network who you admire and ask for advice or collaboration on a project.
- Identify and nurture at least one relationship that can serve as a source of support or accountability in your journey.

CHAPTER TEN

WRITING YOUR SCRIPT, YOUR WAY

The idea of *"writing your script"* always felt a bit dramatic to me, like something out of a motivational seminar where everyone's expected to suddenly reinvent themselves in 24 hours. But here's what I've realized—it's not about tossing your entire life in the air and hoping it lands in a perfect new pattern. It's about picking up the pen, erasing what doesn't feel right, and adding the lines that make you smile

I remember sitting in a café with my friend Arjun (yes, the peanut butter guy). We were sipping overpriced lattes and discussing what we'd do if we could hit a reset button on life. I said I'd travel more and write that book I'd been daydreaming about for years. Arjun, ever the realist, leaned back and said, *"Why do we need a reset button? Can't we just, like, start now?"*

"Start now?" I echoed, raising an eyebrow. *"You sound like a self-help book."*

He grinned. *"Fine, but think about it. Nobody's holding a gun to your head saying, 'Stick to the script you wrote when you were 16.'"*

He had a point. The plans we make when we're younger are often based on what we think we should want—what society, family, or Instagram says is the *"right"* way to live. But as we grow, those plans sometimes stop fitting. It's like wearing a sweater you loved in high school that now feels too tight and scratchy. Why keep wearing it?

The beauty of life is that you're allowed to change your mind. You're allowed to scrap the old script and write a new one—a script that feels more like you.

For me, rewriting my script started with small edits. I stopped saying yes to things that drained me (like that extra *"just for visibility"* project at work) and started saying yes to things that filled me up, like learning to play the guitar.

Spoiler alert: I'm terrible, but strumming a few chords after a long day feels ridiculously good.

One of my favorite edits came during a trip with friends. We were hiking—well, they were hiking; I was mostly panting and regretting my life choices. Somewhere along the trail, my friend Neha joked, *"You're going to write about this someday, aren't you?"*

"Maybe," I said between gasps for air.

"Make sure you leave out the part where I tripped on nothing and fell into that bush," she added with a laugh.

Moments like that reminded me of what I really wanted my script to include: adventures, laughter, and the kind of memories that make you grin years later.

But rewriting your script isn't just about the fun stuff. It's also about confronting the hard truths. I had to admit to myself that some of the things I was holding onto—like certain toxic friendships or unrealistic career goals—weren't serving me anymore. Letting go of those things felt scary, like stepping into the unknown. But it also felt freeing, like clearing out space for something better.

And here's the thing: your script doesn't have to make sense to anyone else. It doesn't have to follow the structure of a *"perfect life"* checklist. It's yours. Want to quit your corporate job and open a tiny coffee shop by the beach? Do it. Want to learn how to salsa dance, even if you have two left feet? Go for it. Want to adopt a cat, name it Sir Purrington, and start a YouTube channel about your adventures? Why not?

Arjun once said, *"The best part about life is that it's not a book. There's no editor telling you, 'Hey, you can't add a dragon in Chapter 5.'"* Okay, maybe dragons aren't a realistic addition, but his point still stands. You're the author, the director, the lead actor—whatever metaphor you prefer.

So, as we wrap up this chapter, let me ask you: What's one line, one scene, one plot twist you'd love to add to your script? Whatever it is, start writing it. The beauty of your script is that it's never truly finished. Every day, every choice, every step forward is a chance to make it more authentically yours.

And if you need a cheerleader along the way, know that I'm rooting for you—bad guitar playing, dragons, and all.

The Art of International Living

Have you ever thought about living in another country—not just visiting, but truly immersing yourself in a different culture? It's not all picture-perfect sunsets and Instagram-worthy moments; it's about embracing the unfamiliar, adapting to new rhythms, and finding beauty in the chaos.

I once laughed when my friend Riya announced, *"I'm moving to Italy because I love pasta."* While her reasoning was questionable, her courage was inspiring. Over time, her stories of navigating tiny markets, learning a new language, and accidentally joining a local parade were proof of how much you grow when you step outside your comfort zone.

Living internationally is a lesson in curiosity and resilience. You learn to find joy in little victories—like mastering public transport or discovering your go-to café. Sure, you'll miss home. I've had my fair share of dramatic rants over missing familiar snacks. But these moments make you resourceful and remind you of the universal kindness that exists everywhere.

So, if you ever get the chance, say yes. Even if it starts small, the experience will shape you in ways you can't imagine. And who knows—you might just come back with more than memories, like a favorite pasta recipe or a new perspective on life.

Practical Steps to Rewrite Your Story

Rewriting your story sounds like one of those self-help clichés, right? But here's the thing: it's actually doable, and surprisingly empowering. Think of your life as a movie script. If a scene isn't working, you don't scrap the whole thing—you rewrite the parts that need fixing.

One of my friends had this habit of turning every conversation into a rant about how life was unfair. *"Bro, if life is so unfair, why not outsmart it?"* I joked one day. That got him thinking. Slowly, he stopped complaining and started acting. He switched jobs, picked up photography on weekends, and now, his Instagram feed looks like National Geographic. He didn't wait for life to get better; he rewrote his role in it.

It starts small. For me, it was about waking up 15 minutes earlier to plan my day. Sounds tiny, but those 15 minutes gave me clarity and a sense of control. Another time, I swapped endless social media scrolling for reading just one page of a book. It wasn't easy—I missed my nightly meme marathons—but the payoff was huge.

What's important is asking yourself: What's one thing I can change today? Maybe it's as simple as saying no to something that drains you or saying yes to an opportunity that scares you. It's not about flipping your life overnight; it's about tweaking it in ways that align with who you want to be.

And when things don't go as planned—because they won't sometimes—laugh about it. I once joined a yoga class to *"redefine my mornings."* Turns out, I redefined falling flat on my face during every pose. But hey, at least I tried.

The beauty of rewriting your story is that it's yours. There's no right or wrong way, no deadlines or grades. Just you, a pen, and a blank page.

Key Takeaways

1. The Art of Intentional Living

- Living intentionally means making conscious decisions that align with your values, goals, and vision for your life.
- By taking responsibility for your choices, you actively create the life you want instead of letting circumstances dictate it.
- Intentional living leads to more fulfillment, purpose, and clarity.

2. Practical Steps to Rewrite Your Story

- Reflect on your past and identify the stories or beliefs that have held you back.
- Rewrite these narratives with a positive, empowering perspective that focuses on growth, resilience, and the future.
- Take actionable steps every day to live in alignment with your new story, no matter how small the changes may seem.

Homework

- Write down one area of your life where you feel stuck or limited. Then, rewrite your story in a way that empowers you to take action and move forward.
- Take one small, intentional step today that reflects your new narrative.

CHAPTER ELEVEN

Staying True to Your Journey

Staying true to yourself—it's a lot harder than it sounds, isn't it? Especially when the world is constantly pulling you in different directions, telling you what you should be doing, wearing, or achieving. I've been there, trying to fit into boxes that weren't even remotely my size. It's exhausting, and frankly, a bit ridiculous.

There was this one time when I joined a marathon just because everyone I knew was doing it. Running isn't my thing—at all. But peer pressure is real. So, I laced up my shoes and showed up. Three minutes in, I was out of breath, questioning all my life choices, while my friends breezed past me like gazelles. By the time I hit the water station, I knew one thing for sure: authenticity is way more important than keeping up with the herd.

Authenticity starts with self-trust. You've got to believe that your instincts and choices are valid, even if they don't align with what's trending. I had a mentor once who said, *"If it doesn't feel right, it's probably not your path."* That stuck with me. It's easy to get swept up in what looks good on the outside, but staying true to your journey means knowing what feels good on the inside.

Reflection helps too. A few years ago, I started keeping a gratitude journal—not the fancy kind with gold-edged pages, just a simple notebook. Every night, I jot down three things that made me smile or feel grateful. Some days it's big things, like landing a project I'd been hoping for. On other days, it's tiny moments, like my coffee being the perfect temperature. That little ritual keeps me grounded and reminds me of what really matters.

Funny story—my friend Arya tried doing the gratitude journal thing too. She's a bit of a rebel, so her entries were less *"thank you for the sunshine"* and more *"grateful I didn't lose my keys today."* But even that worked for her. It's not about how you do it, but that you take a moment to pause and appreciate.

Staying true to your journey is about tuning out the noise and listening to your own voice. It's about trusting that your pace is the right pace and that your path, no matter how winding, is leading you exactly where you need to go. And if you trip along the way, well, that's just another story to laugh about later.

Key Takeaways

- Authenticity is about being true to who you are, even when it's easier to follow others or fit into societal expectations.
- Trust yourself and your instincts, even when the path is unclear. Your intuition is a valuable guide.
- Embrace vulnerability and self-awareness as powerful tools in staying true to your journey.
- Reflection helps you assess how far you've come and what you've learned from your experiences.
- Gratitude shifts your mindset from what's missing to what's already abundant in your life.
- Regular reflection and practicing gratitude foster growth, contentment, and a stronger sense of purpose.

Homework

- Spend 10 minutes each day reflecting on your journey—what have you learned, and how have you stayed true to yourself?
- Write down three things you're grateful for, big or small, and how they contribute to your growth and authenticity.

CHAPTER TWELVE

CREATING YOUR NOW, STARTING TODAY

So here we are, at the end of this little journey together. And if you're thinking, *"This sounds great, but where do I start?"*—don't worry, I've got you. Let's talk about taking action. Not tomorrow, not next week, but today.

First things first, let's drop the idea that you need to overhaul your entire life to see progress. Small steps, my friend. I once read about this concept called the 1% rule—just aim to be 1% better than yesterday. Doesn't that feel manageable? Like, if yesterday you hit snooze five times, maybe today you stop at four. Baby steps.

One of the exercises that really worked for me was listing out just three priorities for the day. Not twenty, not ten. Just three. Back when I started, one of my *"big goals"* was simply to drink more water because, let's be honest, I was running on 90% caffeine. So every morning, I'd write *"Drink 8 glasses of water"* at the top of my list. Did I nail it every time? Nope. But over time, it became second nature.

And speaking of exercises, here's one that's surprisingly fun: set a timer for 10 minutes and write down everything you've been putting off. Big things, small things, even the ridiculous ones like *"finally fix that squeaky cupboard."* When you're done, pick one thing to tackle today. The satisfaction of crossing it off your list? Chef's kiss.

A while ago, my friend Aakash and I tried this exercise together. He looked at his list and said, *"Why does it say 'Call Mom' three times?"* I couldn't stop laughing. Turns out, he'd been avoiding her because she always reminded him about getting married. But you know what? He finally called her, and now she's so happy she's stopped bringing it up. Win-win!

And now, a little pep talk to wrap things up. Wherever you are right now, whatever your circumstances, I want you to know that you can do this. Change doesn't have to be monumental to be meaningful. It's the small, consistent actions that add up over time.

So, start where you are. Take a deep breath, pick one thing, and just begin. Your *"now"* isn't some distant point in the future—it's right here, waiting for you to grab it. And trust me, there's no better time than today.

Thanks for letting me be a part of your journey. Now, go create your amazing now—I'm rooting for you!

Key Takeaways

- Small, intentional actions today can create a ripple effect that transforms your life.
- Start with simple daily habits: write down your goals, break them into small steps, and take action now, not tomorrow.
- Focus on what you can control right now—your attitude, actions, and mindset—rather than waiting for the perfect moment.
- Life is shaped by the choices you make today, not tomorrow. Don't wait for a dramatic moment to start making changes.
- Believe in your ability to create the future you want, one small step at a time.
- Embrace the journey, stay consistent, and remember that every small action leads to significant progress.

Homework

- Choose one small change you can make today to improve your life—whether it's setting a new goal or starting a positive habit.
- Take immediate action—write it down, plan for it, and do it today.
- Reflect on how this simple action makes you feel and how it contributes to creating the future you want.

Acknowledgments: Gratitude To Those Who Inspired This Journey

As I sit down to write this final section, I can't help but smile. This part feels like catching up with an old friend over coffee and saying, "Hey, I couldn't have done this without you." So here goes—my heartfelt thank you to everyone who's been part of this adventure.

First, to my family. You've seen me at my best, my worst, and all the messy in-betweens. To my wife, whose quiet encouragement and endless patience kept me grounded even when I thought I had nothing left to give. And my younger brother, who always knew just when to step in with a joke or a word of wisdom to lift my spirits, even when I didn't know I needed it.

Then there's my circle of friends. You know who you are—the ones who listened to me ramble about this book long before it was even an outline. I mean, how many times can someone ask, "Does this chapter make sense?" without testing a friendship? But you stuck around.

Special shoutout to my buddy, who has been my unofficial sounding board since day one. When I told him I was writing this book, he said, "Oh, so you're finally putting your motivational speeches on paper?" He meant it as a joke, but it's kind of true. Your sarcasm is 50% of the reason I kept going—just to prove you wrong.

And to you, the reader. Yes, you! This book wouldn't exist without the hope that someone, somewhere, might find a little spark of inspiration in these pages. Whether you've laughed, nodded along, or even rolled your eyes at something I've written, thank you for sticking with me. You've been my silent partner in this journey.

Lastly, to life itself. For the challenges, the lessons, the curveballs, and even the "what just happened?" moments. Every bit of it shaped what's here.

So, as I wrap this up, all I can say is thank you. For the encouragement, the tough love, the laughs, and the quiet support that came exactly when I needed it. This journey was never just mine—it was ours.

About The Author: A Glimpse Into My Journey Beyond This Book

Well, if you've made it this far, then I guess you're curious about who I am, beyond just the pages you've been reading. It's a little surreal, really, that we're at this point, but let's get into it—without the formal bio stuff, because who wants that anyway, right?

I'm just a regular person who decided to take some of my experiences— the wins, the failures, the "oops" moments—and share them with you in the hope that it might help you with your own journey. Nothing fancy, just a guy figuring it out as he goes.

So, where do I come from? A place of curiosity, honestly. Ever since I was young, I've been obsessed with learning how things work—whether it was how to fix a bike (which took about ten tries before I finally got it right) or diving deep into books, finding different perspectives on life, success, and happiness. I guess that's how I ended up writing this book. I wanted to see if I could pull together my own experiences and offer something that might help someone else.

It hasn't been a smooth ride, though. I've had my fair share of setbacks and challenges. Like the time I tried to bake a cake for a friend's birthday and ended up with something that looked more like a burnt pancake than anything edible. Needless to say, that wasn't my finest moment in the kitchen, but hey, I'm pretty good at other things, right? Like writing this book, which, let's be honest, was a whole different type of challenge.

But it's not just about failures. There have been moments when I've experienced real growth. When something clicked, I thought, "Okay, this is it. This is the lesson I was meant to learn." And honestly, that's what keeps me going—those moments of clarity and the chance to learn from everything, good or bad.

Outside of writing and all these lessons, I love spending time with my family. They're my foundation. My wife and younger brother are the ones who've been there every step of the way, whether it was to remind me not to stress over every little detail or to share a laugh when I thought something was a big deal (spoiler: it usually wasn't).

Oh, and then there's my passion for learning new things. It's like I can't help myself. Whether it's picking up a new hobby, figuring out how to manage my time better, or just diving into different ways to keep improving, I always have something on my mind. Maybe that's why this book was the natural next step—just another way for me to share what I've learned.

So, what's next for me? Well, I'm still in this process of learning, growing, and evolving. Writing this book is just one chapter (pun intended) in my journey. I don't have it all figured out, and I'm okay with that. Honestly, if I did, I'd probably be bored by now. The whole point is to keep going, keep exploring, and keep sharing what I find along the way.

And who knows, maybe the next book will be about how to not burn a cake—or maybe something else. The point is, I'm just getting started, and I'm really glad you're here for it. So, let's see where this journey takes us.

Thank You

Before you go, I'd like to say thank you for purchasing my book.

You could have picked from dozens of books on mind training, but you took a chance and checked out this one.

So, big thanks for reading this book all the way to the end.

Now I'd like to ask for a small favor. **Could you please take a minute or two and leave a review for this book on Amazon?**

This feedback will help us continue to write the kind of Kindle books that help you get results. And if you love it, please let us know.